Original title:
My Locker's Secret Limericks

Copyright © 2025 Creative Arts Management OÜ
All rights reserved.

Author: Matthew Whitaker
ISBN HARDBACK: 978-3-69074-172-9
ISBN PAPERBACK: 978-3-69074-458-4

Awaiting Discovery Through the Steel

Behind the door with a solid clank,
Lies treasures and snacks, just a prank.
Each time I take a peek,
I giggle and I squeak,
Who knew a pencil could help me with a prank?

Inside there's a note, quite absurd,
With doodles and jokes, how absurd!
A sandwich from last week,
It's past its peak,
But who would dare to disturb?

A rubber duck floats, so bright and round,
A paperclip dragon, big and profound.
With each turn of the key,
It's laughter and glee,
For secrets abound under the mound!

Oh, the chaos locked tight in this place,
Where giggles and grins fill the space.
As friends try to peep,
They fall in a heap—
This locker's a magical space!

Laughter's Capsule in the Classroom

In a corner where shadows might creep,
Lies a barrel of laughs, oh so deep.
When the teacher walks by,
We just can't deny,
These giggles are one secret we keep!

With stickers and toys stacked so high,
We hide novelty cards, oh my!
With each hand that sneaks,
We burst into squeaks,
Creating a ruckus in the shy.

A sock puppet waits with a grin,
To cheer us up when days are dim.
With jokes in its stash,
It brings quite a dash,
Making frowns turn to joy on a whim!

So come gather 'round, my dear friends,
For this fun never really ends.
With secrets galore,
You'll laugh more and more,
In this classroom where laughter transcends!

Rhymes Beneath the Surface

A pencil hiding in the dark,
Proclaims its love for a stray lark.
It scribbles notes at night,
Making the shadows feel quite bright.

An eraser that's seen too much,
Whispers tales, it can't quite touch.
With secrets shared in glee,
They giggle oh-so-quietly.

Laughter's Capsule in the Classroom

In a corner where shadows might creep,
Lies a barrel of laughs, oh so deep.
When the teacher walks by,
We just can't deny,
These giggles are one secret we keep!

With stickers and toys stacked so high,
We hide novelty cards, oh my!
With each hand that sneaks,
We burst into squeaks,
Creating a ruckus in the shy.

A sock puppet waits with a grin,
To cheer us up when days are dim.
With jokes in its stash,
It brings quite a dash,
Making frowns turn to joy on a whim!

So come gather 'round, my dear friends,
For this fun never really ends.
With secrets galore,
You'll laugh more and more,
In this classroom where laughter transcends!

Rhymes Beneath the Surface

A pencil hiding in the dark,
Proclaims its love for a stray lark.
It scribbles notes at night,
Making the shadows feel quite bright.

An eraser that's seen too much,
Whispers tales, it can't quite touch.
With secrets shared in glee,
They giggle oh-so-quietly.

Jokes Told in Quiet Corners

In a nook where whisperers dwell,
A stapler told a tale so swell.
It snapped and clacked with glee,
Creating laughs for you and me.

A highlighter blushed a neon hue,
When told it was the class's glue.
They scribbled all their fears,
Then laughed away the tears.

Laughter from Behind Closed Doors

A notebook penned with wavy lines,
Dreams of donuts and funny signs.
It giggles when it's opened wide,
With doodles from a joyful ride.

A ruler measured all the fun,
It told of races that it won.
With each tick that it made,
Laughter echoed and never strayed.

Mysteries of the Classroom Chamber

A binder full of silly schemes,
Held crazy thoughts and silly dreams.
It caught the whispers like a net,
Of all the laughs that it could get.

A sticky note with a cheeky grin,
Told all the secrets living within.
It fluttered as if to say,
Come laugh with us, it's a great day!

Vaulted Voices of the Unseen

In the depths where whispers play,
A sock sings loud, much to the fray.
Its partner long lost,
In chaos tossed,
Giggles erupt, come what may.

A sandwich remains, oddly bright,
In this vault of pure delight.
Pickles and cheese,
Bring friends to their knees,
Guffaws spring forth, soaring light.

Scribbles of Laughter in Hiding

On crumpled sheets with doodles grand,
There lies a tale, carefully planned.
A cat with a crown,
In a jester's gown,
Makes the squirrels all take a stand.

An eraser bolted quick,
Turns out to be quite the trick.
It hides from the rest,
In a pencil's nest,
Creating a laughter so sick.

The Enchanted Frame of Jokes

Inside a frame of silver shine,
Are jokes that are simply divine.
A pun on a wall,
Makes everyone fall,
Clutching their sides, oh so fine!

A rubber chicken gleams with pride,
In this world where chuckles collide.
It hops, it flops,
As laughter stops,
In a burst where silliness hides.

Hidden Melodies and Giggling Verse

In corners where giggles arise,
A melody flutters, oh what a surprise!
A tune on the loose,
With rhymes to produce,
Makes everyone laugh till they cry.

A whoopee cushion, cheeky and bold,
Tells stories of laughter, never old.
With each little squeak,
The laughter gets peak,
An age-old delight to behold.

The Playful Prose Hidden Within

In a box with a twist and a turn,
Lies a note filled with jokes that I yearn.
When I find it in glee,
Laughter waits just for me,
And silly old tales take their churn.

A banana once danced on a shelf,
Claiming it needed some help.
With a chuckle and grin,
It pulled off a win,
And soon, all the fruit joined itself.

Whimsical Whispers in Alloy

Behind metal doors, laughter flows,
Jokes and puns in a clever prose.
A rubber chicken sings,
Of all silly things,
Where each line tickles and glows.

In the corners, some socks tell a tale,
Of the time they went out on a sail.
With a wink and a cheer,
They spread joy far and near,
While leaving us clutching our quail.

The Quirky Collection Behind Bars

A squirrel once wrote me a note,
It claimed to have learned how to float.
With a splash and a cheer,
It danced round the beer,
And left all the mice quite remote.

In my stash lies a shoe with a hat,
It wobbles and dances like that.
When I open the door,
It goes for a tour,
And makes all my friends keep it flat.

Stashed Sonnets and Puns

An old book filled with rhymes that entice,
Teaches dogs how to play pretty nice.
With a wag and a bark,
They jump in the park,
And make quite the wonderful slice.

I once hid a shoe that could sing,
And it fancied itself to be bling.
With each tender note,
It got mice to gloat,
As it wore a bright glittery ring.

Hidden Humor and Rhyming Bliss

In a chest where giggles hide,
A rubber chicken's by my side.
The socks are odd,
The puns are broad,
Mischief greets me like a guide.

There's crayons of every hue,
And jellybeans, sticky and blue.
A magic wand,
With jokes so grand,
This place is pure laughter's view.

The Encrypted Joy of Playful Words

Within these walls, I keep my jest,
With tickles and giggles, I am blessed.
A whoopee cushion,
A secret mission,
This treasure chest puts humor to the test.

A riddle wrapped in a joke,
In shadows where the giggles poke.
Each note a quirk,
With laughter's perk,
These playful whispers I invoke.

Secrets of the Silly Sage

The wise old sage in socks so bright,
Whispers tales that bring delight.
A rubber bat,
It's quite a chat,
In this secret spot, joy takes flight.

With mischievous grins, I share my finds,
A pirate hat that mischievously binds.
With every clue,
Another laugh too,
In this wacky world where fun unwinds.

The Jesters' Keepsake in Concealment

A jester's hat of colors bright,
Hides chuckles deep inside at night.
With silly baubles,
And playful troubles,
Each secret joke ignites delight.

Behind this door, the laughter swells,
In whispers, every humor dwells.
My trinkets sing,
On joyous wing,
In this stash where fun excels.

Tales Tucked in the Back

Behind the door, a tale is spun,
Of rubber bands and bubble gum.
A paper plane that flew too high,
Landed in the math book, oh my!

A secret stash of silly notes,
With drawings of odd, floating boats.
Each one a giggle, a daft surprise,
For every student, a sweet reprise.

The Camouflaged Cadence of Play

In corners where the ruckus thrives,
A jingle lingers, that's when it jives.
A hidden laugh, a pulse that springs,
From shoelace pranks and paper rings.

Whispers echo in every nook,
A ticklish tale inside the book.
With every shift and shuffle done,
The joy erupts, it's all in fun!

Lighthearted Mischief from Afar

Across the room, a giggle bursts,
As pencils dance and the mischief flirts.
Sticky notes fly with glee so bright,
Creating chaos, what a sight!

Inventive plots in secret hide,
A sneaky prank, we laugh and bide.
In shadows cast by morning light,
The fun unfolds, oh what a night!

Secrets in the Stanza Chamber

In hush-hush tones, the verses sing,
Bringing delight with every swing.
A giggled rhyme, a whispered jest,
In clever lines, we find our rest.

Each folded paper, a treasure kept,
With playful secrets softly crept.
A heart that races, a laugh we share,
In this chamber, laughter fills the air!

Glistening Words in the Unknown

In a locker there lies a tale,
With whispers and giggles that sail.
A sock with a grin,
And a pen full of sin,
Where each secret brings laughter, not pale.

Among pencils, a note takes its flight,
A joke that can tease day and night.
With each little prank,
From paper to blank,
The echoes of laughter ignite.

Secrets of the Scholar's Haven

Behind every book, there's a laugh,
A riddle that splits in half.
With each little clue,
It tickles me too,
In this haven of scholarly guffaw.

A sandwich, a joke, and some cheer,
Hidden treasures just waiting near.
An apple gone bad,
But oh, it's not mad,
For laughter is what we hold dear.

Lyrical Mysteries Buried Deep

The bottom drawer hides all the fun,
Where lyrics and giggles can run.
A rubber band ball,
And rhymes for us all,
Compose a symphony under the sun.

With crayons and doodles so bright,
Each scribble ignites pure delight.
A secretive winks,
And whimsical thinks,
Transform this plain space into light.

The Counter of Comedic Counts

In a locker, jokes stack to the brim,
Each punchline makes serious dim.
When counting the beads,
Or laughing at deeds,
These comedic counts never grow grim.

With giggles that bounce off the wall,
A story unfolds, oh so tall.
A tickle, a roll,
In every small hole,
This chaos we cherish, enthrall!

The Enigma in the Hallway

In a hall, there's a door so sly,
With whispers and giggles nearby.
A note made of cheese,
Brings students to knees,
As laughter spreads wide in the sky.

A sock from a shoe left behind,
Held secrets, so funny, aligned.
It bounced like a ball,
In the echoing hall,
Where mysteries, silly, unwind.

Scribbles of a Secret Keeper

On paper, a doodle resided,
With seas of confetti beside it.
A cat in a hat,
Chasing after a rat,
In laughter, the whole class divided.

With jokes hidden deep in the lines,
Of pranks and of silly designs.
A fish with a tie,
Makes everyone cry,
As humor through each corner shines.

Echoes in the Halls of Youth

In the halls, echoes bounce with delight,
Where children make mischief take flight.
A banana peel flung,
While giggling is sung,
Is it chaos or simply goodnight?

With sneakers that squeak and they squeal,
The tales that each corner can steal.
A ghost made of fluff,
Could never be tough,
But tickles the hearts that reveal.

The Hidden Humor Within

Within pages, such wonders reside,
With giggles and snorts that collide.
A frog wearing pants,
In a dance-filled expanse,
Wrapping up all the grins far and wide.

The best-kept surprise in a drawer,
Is a rubber chicken galore.
It cackles and clucks,
In its antics, it lucks,
Leaving everyone craving for more.

Whispers of Clever Quips

In a room where giggles hide,
A monkey swings from side to side.
He juggles socks with glee,
And tickles you for free.

With each laugh, the secrets slide,
As silly treasures bide.
A rubber chicken's there,
To add to the playful air.

Lying low, a whoopee pie,
Makes every serious sigh.
It winks with whipped delight,
Turning gloom into a flight.

So come and lend an ear,
To laughter held so dear.
These whispers, oh so bright,
Will chase away the night.

Scraps of Silly Stories

Once a cat wore a little hat,
Who thought it was a fancy mat.
It slipped, and what a sight,
She danced in pure delight.

A turtle painted on a spree,
Declared, "I'm fast, just wait and see!"
But tripped over his shell,
And rang a funny bell.

There's also a frog, quite spry,
Who sings as he hops on by.
His voice, a croaky tune,
Makes flowers dance by noon.

Each tale is wrapped in giggles,
As laughter just wiggles.
These scraps, they never tire,
In a world that's full of fire.

The Hidden Haven of Humor

In a corner, joy resides,
With jokes and puns like tides.
A squirrel cracks a grin,
As the laughter flows in.

A pickle dressed in bright attire,
Claims it's the world's best liar.
Meanwhile, a bee buzzes loud,
Singing with its buzzing crowd.

There's a fish that tells a tale,
Of sailing ships and a gale.
Every splash brings a cheer,
To those who gather near.

In this haven, smiles don't hide,
They leap and dance with pride.
Humor's glow, brightly spun,
Unites us, everyone.

Verses of the Unseen

Behind the door, a riddle waits,
With rubber ducks and silly plates.
They whisper jokes divine,
In a world that feels benign.

A phantom wears mismatched socks,
And laughs at all the ticking clocks.
It tiptoes with a glee,
Dancing 'round, come look and see!

In shadows lurk some funny pets,
Each one with jokes like no regrets.
Their antics fill the air,
With giggles everywhere.

These verses float like fluffs of cream,
In a world of humor's dream.
So join the fun, let's play,
In this light-hearted ballet.

Whispers from the Hidden Shelf

There once was a sock with a gaze,
It told all the secrets of days.
With each little giggle,
It made my heart wiggle,
And danced in a curious haze.

A pencil would scribble in glee,
While hidden from all eyes to see.
With lines so absurd,
It spoke every word,
Of a cat that climbed up a tree.

Each paperclip had a bold tale,
Of adventures on a grand scale.
They'd twist and they'd bend,
With laughter they send,
As they journeyed across a bright trail.

So peek behind doors ever so sly,
Where oddities giggle and fly.
A treasure awaits,
With whimsical fates,
As secrets await with a sigh.

The Vault of Silenced Rhymes

In a box where the papers lay neat,
A stapler could dance to a beat.
It whirred with delight,
From morning to night,
Creating a symphony sweet.

An eraser once plotted a scheme,
To vanish each pencil's grand dream.
With nibbles and bites,
It caused silly fights,
Turning scribbles to wisps in a beam.

Behind those dull walls, life did thrive,
With laughter and joy, we'd arrive.
The paperclip crew,
Had antics anew,
Making every dull moment alive.

If you shuffle and shuffle around,
Many wonders could surely be found.
So tiptoe and peek,
For joy that you seek,
In the vault where the quirks are unbound.

Enigmatic Verses Behind Closed Doors

A notepad held stories so wild,
Of dreams told by a curious child.
With doodles and scribes,
It laughed as it bribes,
The shy little thoughts that are filed.

There's a binder that loves to confide,
With secrets it never could hide.
With ruffles and folds,
It whispers bold,
And spins tales that twinkle with pride.

A rubber band stretched ever so far,
Played jump rope with fate like a star.
It bounced with a grin,
Inviting us in,
To hop over ink, near and far.

Behind locked drawers, let stories unwind,
With quirky delights that you'll find.
So chuckle away,
Through a whimsical day,
Of wonders that twist in your mind.

The Mysterious Stanzas of Innocence

A crayon once drew a tall tale,
Of pirate ships caught in a gale.
With swirls and with curls,
It took off like twirls,
Setting sail on a rainbow trail.

A glue stick decided to sing,
Creating the wildest of things.
With sticky delight,
It held dreams so bright,
As joy in a bottle it brings.

Each sticker held laughter galore,
With smiles and with giggles in store.
They'd shuffle and play,
In a fun, silly way,
And stick to my heart evermore.

So peek into boxes of cheer,
For creatures that giggle and leer.
The stanzas await,
In a whimsical state,
With secrets that dance ever near.

Quips and Quirks Under Lock and Key

In a place where secrets reside,
Lies a treasure, wide-eyed and spry.
A banana peel with a smile,
Makes even tough days worthwhile.

Among the pens and old snacks,
There's a note that loudly cracks.
"Why did the book feel so shy?"
"Because it had too many issues to try!"

The Giggling Fragments of Youth

Tucked away in a dusty drawer,
Lies laughter, like never before.
A hidden stash of candy bars,
And silly jokes from near and far.

A rubber chicken, broken but bold,
Tells tales of mischief, never old.
"Why don't scientists trust a stair?"
"Because it's always up to something, beware!"

Witty Whispers in the Quiet

In the silence, there's a peek,
Of giggles playing hide and seek.
A whoopee cushion makes a sound,
As laughter bounces all around.

Post-it notes with jokes to share,
Little treasures tucked with care.
"How do you organize a space party?"
"You planet!" Oh, the joy is hearty!

Shadows of Humor in Steel Walls

Within these walls of cold, hard steel,
Lies a comic treasure, so surreal.
A tiny frog with a silly hat,
Croaks out jokes, imagine that!

Behind the lock, whispers float,
Of silly pranks and a joke remote.
"What did the zero say to the eight?"
"Nice belt!" Ah, laughter can't wait!

Jests Embodied by Bound Pages

In a corner, I found a surprise,
A notebook of jokes in disguise.
Each page full of laughter,
With puns and some banter.

A frog and a squirrel had a fight,
Their antics were quite a delight.
They bounced and they croaked,
While everyone joked.

One liners and chuckles so grand,
In my secret stash, they all stand.
I read them with glee,
What a sight to see!

So if you're in need of a cheer,
Just whisper a joke in your ear.
These pages, they play,
In the silliest way!

The Compartment of Comical Chants

In a drawer where the papers are stacked,
A treasure of giggles is packed.
Small notes with big laughs,
Crafted by silly crafts.

The cat wore a hat, oh so bright,
It danced and it jived with delight.
A mouse in a shoe,
What antics they do!

With every dumb joke, I can't stop,
Why did the chicken? Oh, it's top!
These comics ignite,
Pure joy in the night.

So dive into this stash of delight,
Where laughter can soar to new height.
Just open the bind,
And let joy unwind!

Riddles of the Closed Space

In the shadows, where quirks intertwine,
A ledger of giggles, so fine.
Riddles that tease,
Like a soft summer breeze.

What runs but never can walk?
I found that old, funny talk.
The answers come quick,
With a humorous trick.

A riddle to ponder and share,
In this compartment, they're rare.
With a giggle, I sigh,
As the day flutters by.

So bring out your senses of play,
In this nook, let's shout hooray!
The riddles are here,
To spark all the cheer!

Secrets of Syllables Stowed Away

Within some folds where the whispers go,
Lurk secrets that put on a show.
Each syllable dressed,
In humor it's best.

A penguin once slipped on some ice,
And laughed as he fell, oh so nice!
He rolled and he tumbled,
Around all he fumbled.

Just lines that bring chuckles to light,
In the quiet, they spark pure delight.
So read if you dare,
For laughter you'll wear!

The syllables dance in the dark,
Each story ignites a fun spark.
So open the page,
And set the fun stage!

Poetry Concealed in Lockdown

In the corner where whispers reside,
A rhyme sneaks out, trying to hide.
An ode to lost socks,
And shoes with warped knocks.

Giggles emerge from behind the steel,
As verses spin tales they conceal.
A pencil at play,
In a mischievous way.

Lines that dance like a cat on the floor,
Chasing shadows, then hiding once more.
In this fortress of fun,
The laughter can run.

A riddle unwound, like a spring,
Each joke flickers, ready to sing.
With a tickle of rhyme,
And a dash of good time.

Limericks in the Shadowed Chamber

In a box where dark secrets ignite,
A rhyme takes its playful flight.
A frog in a hat,
Calls the cat just to chat.

Giggles roar as the shadows meet,
A limerick simmers, oh so sweet.
Why did the shoe,
Dance with a zoo?

In this chamber, plots twist and twine,
A jabbering verse, oh so fine.
With a wink and a grin,
They all skip right in.

While shadows cast shapes, curious and odd,
The laughter weaves tales, oh it's broad.
A tickle of word,
In the dark it absurd!

The Clutch of Cleverness

Behind the doors, where secrets lie,
A pun lands softly, oh my!
A beetle in disguise,
Wears spectacles, oh what a surprise!

With a wink, he recites his best,
In this crafty little nest.
Why did the worm,
Take a turn?

Tales of wisdom, odd and bright,
Flow from the shadows, sheer delight.
A twist of the tongue,
Makes laughter well sprung.

In cleverness' clutch, tales unfold,
As laughter's warmth, bright and bold.
So come take a peek,
At this playful feat.

Concocted Chronicles in Darkness

In a crevice where giggles reside,
A story of chaos and pride.
A sandwich that danced,
With peanut butter pranced.

In darkness, concoctions are made,
With humor and joy tightly laid.
A pickle in boots,
With marvelous roots.

Verses emerge from an unseen door,
Whispering tales forevermore.
Why did the lemon,
Become a true gem?

Chronicled laughs in a paper-thin line,
Where each word doth truly shine.
In shadows we play,
As jokes pave the way.

Rhyme and Reason

In a box that holds quite a tale,
There's a sock with a weird little frail.
It dances and twirls,
With glittery swirls,
A fashion show for a snail.

A peanut butter sandwich inside,
Decided to take a wild ride.
It slipped on a shoe,
A bus and a stew,
And now it can't seem to abide.

Wrapped Tight

There's a sandwich wrapped snug like a hug,
With a pickle all snug as a bug.
It whispers, "Oh dear,
I've filled up with cheer,
Though I'm starting to smell like a rug!"

A lollipop sitting right there,
With a flavor that's sweet as a dare.
It dreams of the day,
In a parade, it will sway,
While everyone stops to just stare.

Stanzas in Secret Compartments

A collection of notes made with glee,
Finds a rhythm that's funny and free.
With each clever rhyme,
It dances through time,
Creating a giggling spree.

Beneath books of math and of art,
There's a treasure that's set to depart.
A rubber duck flies,
In a whimsy disguise,
And it's headed straight for the heart!

The Untold Tales of Textbooks

A history book, dusty and old,
Hides secrets and stories untold.
With a flip and a spin,
Like a dance in the din,
It reveals a great treasure of gold.

The science text fumbles and plays,
With a beaker that bubbles and sways.
It dreams of a show,
Where the formulas flow,
And everyone laughs through the haze.

Whimsy Behind the Lock

Behind a door, a pencil takes flight,
In a world where the erasers unite.
They gather in packs,
With colorful snacks,
Planning pranks that feel just right.

A note that's been crumpled, now bold,
Spills confessions of dreams left untold.
It giggles and brags,
In its paper bag,
With a heart full of stories to unfold.

The Silenced Bards Beneath the Surface

In a nook where whispers dwell,
A bard with a secret to tell.
His rhymes grew stout,
But no one's about,
Laughing softly, his stories compel.

He tickled the dust on the floor,
While mops danced and begged for encore.
His jokes went unseen,
Like a prank on the bean,
Yet echoes of giggles still soar.

Through shadows, he jotted his wit,
In a place that was cramped and quite lit.
The rift of the day,
In odd shades of gray,
Brought smiles from a tune we can't quit.

For each silly line, we still seek,
In locked drawers, the jovial peak.
His whimsy we find,
With laughter entwined,
Glimmers bright from a joyous antique.

Cryptic Cheer from a Forgotten Place

In corners where dust bunnies play,
A jester's pen scribbles away.
His secrets abound,
In silence profound,
Where ticklish thoughts frolic and sway.

Each note hides a chuckle or two,
Written fast and stuck like a glue.
Old gum stuck around,
With jokes tightly bound,
In a pit where the silly winds blew.

The curtains of mirth softly swing,
As whispers of giggles take wing.
With riddles of yore,
Behind a closed door,
Lies a chorus of laughter we bring.

For every nutty little tale,
There's a sly grin, never to fail.
In shadows, it gleams,
With whimsical dreams,
A treasure map, laughter's own trail.

Laughter's Vault: Rhymes of Revelation

In a vault where the laughter does drip,
A treasure of chuckles does slip.
Jokes sealed tight in a seal,
And gags made of meal,
Prompting fits of joy on each trip.

The rhymes do a jig in the dark,
Amidst echoes, you'll hear their sharp bark.
Each punchline misplaced,
In a snickered haste,
Is artfully weaved like a spark.

An alchemist of jest, so grand,
Where the whispers of humor do stand.
With a quirk and a pun,
Like the pop of a gun,
He conjures a laugh with a hand.

So peek at the wall and you'll see,
The giggles enchanted with glee.
They wiggle and whirl,
In a whimsical curl,
Unlocking a tide of esprit.

Lines of Laughter in Disguise

In a drawer with a lock full of smiles,
A collection of riffs and wild styles.
Hidden jokes softly croon,
Like a full afternoon,
Playing tricks that last for miles.

Each scrap has a wink, quite misplaced,
With humor that's goofy, yet laced.
Banana peels post,
And ticklish toast,
Lead to laughter swirled and embraced.

A mosaic of giggles tucked tight,
In a crevice that teases the night.
With quirks and quick jests,
Laughter surely rests,
Waiting just for the right little bite.

So let's unlock the joyous refrain,
With each giggle bound to entertain.
In whispers so bright,
They dance in the light,
Bringing joy from the depths of plain.

The Vault of Laughter

In a box with jokes galore,
I find gags I can't ignore.
With a tickle and a grin,
They jump out like they've sinned.

A rubber chicken takes a bow,
Declaring, "You can't beat me now!"
It flaps and flops in my hand,
Spreading joy throughout the land.

Here's a riddle—what's a frog?
A ribbeting friend, or a cog?
Laughter echoes in this space,
As smiles light up each face.

With pranks tucked inside this hide,
There's mischief I cannot abide.
When the bell rings, it's no surprise,
Joy bursts forth and never dies.

Encrypted Rhymes in Steel

Behind the door, a treasure's feel,
A stash of rhymes with playful zeal.
Each scribbled note, a chuckling tease,
Guaranteed to bring you to your knees.

A pun that spins like a yo-yo,
Makes classmates laugh, and then they glow.
Why did the cookie go to school?
To get a little smart, it's the rule!

Secrets wrapped in giggles, tight,
Mischief dances day and night.
A jellybean, a trickster, too,
Daring you to laugh anew!

A whoopee cushion's cheeky sound,
Makes a grand joke go round and round.
With each grin, the code unwinds,
Creating joy that surely binds.

The Humor That Binds

Inside the safe, the chuckles hide,
A world of laughter, full of pride.
With a wink, it taps my shoulder,
Reminding me that fun grows bolder.

A pirate walked into a school,
With a parrot perched—oh, what a fool!
He quirked, "I'm here to steal your hearts!"
And everyone burst out with hearty starts.

With notes of mirth stacked to the top,
It's hard for my giggles to stop.
Each rhyme, a candy, sweet and bright,
Spreading joy, like stars at night.

In this chamber filled with cheer,
Jokes ripen perfectly each year.
The bonds we share, so snug and tight,
Illuminate the darkest night.

Echoes of Youthful Banter

Within these walls, the laughter flows,
From silly tales that everyone knows.
A cat that danced, a dog that sang,
Each little quip makes my heart clang.

Who's the king of the awkward pause?
It's the person who shuffles without cause!
With jokes that flip, and puns that sway,
We circle round to hear the play.

The echo of a giggle's trace,
Reminds me of every friendly face.
From knock-knock jokes to tales of woe,
In echoes of laughter, we all grow.

A snack that drops, a soda spray,
Funny moments that refuse to fray.
In this realm of jokes and cheer,
Youthful banter rings ever clear.

Rhymes from the Depths of Steel

In a binder that's full of delight,
I found a surprise in the night.
With a giggle and cheer,
I read from the sphere;
Limericks that took off in flight.

A pencil was stuck in the groove,
Wiggling, it started to move.
It scribbled a tale,
Of a fish with a sail,
As if it was trying to prove.

So I chuckled and rolled with the fun,
While pizza dreams danced in the sun.
Each rhyme spilled out quickly,
Oh, so very slickly,
Who knew my notebook could run?

In the depths, where shadows come play,
Lies humor that brightens the day.
With pen in my hand,
I'll take my grand stand,
And share all the laughs on display.

The Enchanted Locker

Once a locker, so plain and so gray,
Hid treasures that sparkled like clay.
With a jingle, a shush,
And a whimsical hush,
It laughed as I opened the way.

Inside were some notes full of glee,
And a rubber band, wild and free.
A pickle on skates,
And some funny debates,
All waiting to tickle with glee.

My friends gathered round, eyes aglow,
As the laughter began to overflow.
With every new rhyme,
It felt just like time,
Would dance and parade in a show.

To discover the magic laid bare,
With humor that floated on air.
Each giggle a sound,
A joy to be found,
In the locker that held all my care.

Locket of Limericks

Tucked inside a small, shiny box,
I found some odd socks and a fox.
With a grin on his face,
He danced all over the place,
While cracking up jokes like a hoax.

This locket, so small yet so grand,
Brought giggles that filled up the land.
With a flip of a page,
It turned the dull stage,
Into laughter, all perfectly planned.

Each verse tickled toes, made hearts leap,
As we giggled and grinned in a heap.
The silly parade,
In shade or in glade,
With limericks nestled, so deep.

Oh, the joy that it brings to this day,
With humor that's clever and play.
So I'll keep it real bright,
Sharing laughter at night,
For the smiles that never fade away.

The Hidden Cache of Comedy

Behind a good locker, well hashed,
A treasure of humor was stashed.
With a wink and a grin,
The punchlines jumped in,
As laughter and giggles all crashed.

There were poems of frogs in top hats,
And kittens who juggled with bats.
With a chorus of cheer,
The jokes drew us near,
As we rolled on the floor with the cats.

What a riot it was, pure delight,
As we battled through jokes that felt light.
With each silly quip,
Our sides began to slip,
In a whirlwind of giggles one night.

So I treasure this stash, oh so bright,
For 'neath all that charm lies pure light.
Each rhyme holds a key,
To the fun, wild and free,
In the locker that beams with delight.

Poems Stashed in Quiet Confines

In corners where whispers tend to creep,
Lies a stash of rhymes that never sleep.
With jokes that tease and puns that play,
These silly verses brighten the day.

A rhyme about a cat with big dreams,
Who hitches a ride on a skateboard's gleam.
He flips and flops, then lands on his face,
Yet still wears a grin, full of grace.

Old sneakers dancing in a strange parade,
With socks mismatched, a colorful charade.
They twirl and spin, then trip on a line,
Making all of us laugh till we whine.

So come take a peek, don't be shy,
These playful poems are just a sly guy.
Unlock laughter, unlock a surprise,
In the quiet corners, joy never dies.

Verses Veiled in Silence

Within shadows where giggles softly play,
A treasure of verses quietly lay.
Like cupcakes sprouting from a bland, gray plot,
Each line twinkles with mischief, quite a lot.

A squirrel on a swing, quite the sight,
Flipping his tail, oh what a flight!
He swings so high, thinks he's a bird,
But all hear a thud, not a single word.

An old eraser with a heart so true,
Dreams of being a rocket, flying through blue.
It soars past the notebook, oh so proud,
Till it's caught in the hair of a dreamy crowd.

A riddle hidden beneath a book's layer,
Makes friends chuckle, what player, what player!
With humor tucked snug, in spaces we keep,
These verses veiled wake laughter from sleep.

Hidden Sonnets of the School

In a desk that creaks with every lean,
Lie sonnets disguised as a chocolate sheen.
With every verse, a giggle disguises,
Crafted cleverly, tucked in surprises.

A playful pup in a spelling bee,
Whispers the words, "I just want to be!"
Instead, he barks, and the crowd bursts out,
The judge rolls his eyes—what's that about?

A pencil that twirls with grace and flair,
Dreams of the stage, a star beyond compare.
It jots down laughs, it slides like a breeze,
Bringing forth smiles with such gentle ease.

So peek in the shadows, don't miss the fun,
These hidden sonnets bring joy, everyone!
With grins that twinkle like stars of the night,
They'll brighten your day, oh what a delight!

Limericks in Lurking Places

In a nook where no one dares to peek,
Lurks a limerick with a twist and a sneak.
Tales of a hamster that learned how to skate,
His wobbly dance, oh what a fate!

A bird with a hat, quite absurd indeed,
Wants to be a detective, full of speed.
With magnifying glasses and a quirky air,
He searches for crumbs, but finds only hair!

In lockers and books, the whispers abound,
Of goofy rhymes that spin round and round.
They tickle our sides, bring us into fits,
With laughter like waves, they cover our wits.

So gather around, unfold the delight,
Limericks cuddled, ready to ignite.
In those lurking places, mirth takes a stance,
Join the fun, take a chance in the dance!

Rhyme-Riddled Realms

In a chamber of laughs and glee,
Books dance like they just want to be.
A sock hops with flair,
While a pen does declare,
"This isn't your typical spree!"

A sandwich from two weeks ago,
Is ripe with a new kind of glow.
It winks with a grin,
Saying, "Let's dive in!"
But I think I will leave it below.

The gum stuck to keys starts to sing,
Of grapefruits and lovebirds in spring.
It's sticky but nice,
Like a roll of hot spice,
And chuckles it joyfully brings.

In this treasure of mismatched delight,
Mysteries hide out of sight.
Each trinket a laugh,
On this bizarre path,
Where nonsense takes flight through the night.

Banter Behind the Shield

Behind my door, secrets lay,
Jokes and odd socks come to play.
A ruler styled bold,
With stories retold,
Tells tales of a mischievous day.

A paperclip bent on a quest,
Claims titles among all the rest.
Between giggles and dread,
It draws brains on my head,
While I offer it popcorn for zest.

A turtle-shaped eraser so wise,
Watches with narrow-set eyes.
It whispers to me,
"Come and see!"
Cutouts of blue skies contrive.

There's humor in every small crevice,
Each piece tells a story, so generous.
In shadows of light,
Each wrong feels so right,
As laughter finds refuge in this.

Limericks Laid to Rest

In corners all dusty yet bright,
Live limericks waiting for flight.
A folder with flair,
Guarding giggles with care,
Dreams blossoming under moonlight.

There once was a cat in a hat,
Who fancied himself quite the brat.
He'd strut down the hall,
Then trip and then sprawl,
While joking to all, "Is that flat?"

Old marbles roll tales of the past,
With whizzes and booms that will last.
They tumble and chase,
With style and some grace,
Guarding legends with every cast.

In a drawer full of secrets galore,
Hugs from a teddy bear's core.
It's all fun and games,
Where nothing's the same,
In a realm where you're never a bore.

The Insider's Delight

Enter a world quite absurd,
Where nonsense is often preferred.
A comb sings a tune,
As wide as the moon,
Making hairdos excitedly stirred.

A pencil with doodles so grand,
Sketches monsters that prance on command.
With each laugh it creates,
A new joke it elates,
In this whimsical, wild wonderland.

A crumpled-up note teases fate,
It winks at the door, can't wait.
"Try reading my lines,
Or dancing in twines,
This madness is surely first rate!"

With treasures and giggles in tow,
Every secret prepares for a show.
In this delightful place,
Where absurd dreams embrace,
The fun never seems to slow.

The Fun Beneath the Surface

In a world where odd things hide,
A sandwich made for a wild ride.
With pickles and cheese,
It sparked quite a tease,
Causing giggles we just can't bide.

A note from a friend was found,
Whispering secrets all around.
With each scribbled word,
More laughter occurred,
As memories joyful were bound.

Old gum perched on the door's edge,
Was once a bold, sticky pledge.
A treasure in there,
With stories to share,
Brings smiles from the past's simple dredge.

From crayons and toys to a shoe,
Each item holds laughter anew.
With treasures like this,
It's hard to miss,
The joy that comes from the view.

Tales Trapped in Time

A rubber band with a twisty curl,
Once shot at a boy with a whirl.
It zoomed through the air,
Oh, what a scare,
As laughter began to unfurl.

A sticker stuck fast on the wall,
Claims victory over the fall.
It shimmers and shines,
In all of its lines,
As echoes of childhood enthrall.

A paper crane folded with care,
Stuck beneath an old school chair.
It flutters and flaps,
Imitating saps,
Bringing giggles beyond compare.

Old lunch notes with doodles in ink,
Make everyone stop and think.
With jokes packed inside,
They become our pride,
Turning frowns into smiles in a blink.

Giggles Encased in Metal

A funny keychain jingles bright,
And dances in the morning light.
It laughs as it swings,
While joyfully sings,
Of memories that spark pure delight.

A compass that leads us astray,
Points left when we wanted to play.
But in every wrong turn,
There's laughter to learn,
As we find our own silly way.

A little mirror reflects our face,
With silly grins, it finds its place.
It shows all the fun,
Underneath the sun,
As we share in our goofy embrace.

A small lock with a riddle near,
Holds secrets that bring us good cheer.
In moments we find,
It's laughter, not blind,
That keeps every memory clear.

Mysterious Melodies of Youth

A whistle hidden deep inside,
Plays tunes that we used to hide.
With each little note,
Emotions do float,
Reminding us of youthful pride.

A poem scribbled on a page,
But it's more than what's on the stage.
Its riddles unfold,
As the laughter grows bold,
Igniting our inner child's rage.

A toy drum that beats on its own,
Resonates with a cheeky tone.
As we tap and we play,
It echoes the sway,
Of all the fun we have known.

With memories wrapped in a song,
We remember where we belong.
They dance in our hearts,
As each laughter starts,
A chorus of laughter so strong.

Jests and Secrets in Steel

In a box of silver gleams,
I hide my wildest dreams.
With notes that wiggle and dance,
They laugh as I take a chance.

Gags scribbled on crumpled sheets,
Laughter erupts, oh what feats!
Each joke is a playful poke,
In a world where we all choke.

A riddle meant to confuse,
Left behind just to amuse.
When friends come to share a grin,
They find where the fun begins.

So come take a peek inside,
Where secrets and giggles collide.
In the thrumming heart of steel,
Lies a treasure that's all too real.

Limericks in the Shadows

There once was a joke quite obscure,
Tucked away, it became pure.
With each rhyme's funny twist,
Laughter no one could resist,
In shadows they danced, that's for sure.

A limerick twisted with flair,
Sprung forth from a deep hidden lair.
It tickled and teased,
Left all in stitches, pleased,
As giggles filled up the stale air.

An odd rhyme crafted in glee,
Whirling around like a bee.
In laughter's embrace,
We all found our place,
Unraveling jokes over tea.

So whisper the lines of delight,
Let humor take wing in the night.
In shadows, we'll share,
Those limericks rare,
And revel in giggles so bright.

The Covert Collection of Cheer

Hidden treasures lay in a heap,
A silly stash buried deep.
With puns that brightly gleam,
Each one a whimsical dream.

A giggle wrapped tight in a fold,
A tale of a cat, brave and bold.
With each turn of phrase,
Laughter enters a haze,
As joy starts to break through the cold.

They say laughter is good for the soul,
So gather around, let's make it our goal.
With quirks and with quips,
We'll take playful trips,
And let every secret unroll.

So open the box, take a peek,
Find laughter, not answers you seek.
In a world of delight,
Where jokes take their flight,
We'll dance 'til the morning is bleak.

Misfit Lines Beneath the Surface

Down where the odd jokes reside,
Misfit lines often confide.
With whispers and grins,
The laughter begins,
Unveiling what's kept deep inside.

A riddle that twists and turns,
For humor, our spirit yearns.
Each word falls in line,
A play so divine,
A mess full of giggles and burns.

With scribbles and doodles galore,
Each pun is a playful encore.
In circles we weave,
As laughter we cleave,
Unlocking the joy at our core.

So join in the fun with glee,
As we toast to our quirky spree.
In misfit lines shared,
Our laughter's declared,
A funny, bright melody!

The Keeper of Stanzas

In a corner where pencils confide,
Lies a diary where giggles reside.
It holds all my plots,
And humor in knots,
That tickle my brain and provide.

With riddles and jests so obscure,
Each line's a new prank I secure.
A tale of a cat,
That danced with a hat,
And made all the mice feel unsure.

When friends gather 'round for a laugh,
They scour each page like a graph.
Each stanza unfolds,
With gags worth their gold,
Turning snorts into fits on the path.

So here's to my stanzas so bright,
They bring joy as I write them each night.
With giggles in tow,
I let humor flow,
Creating sweet chaos in flight.

Verse Locked Away

Behind a door rusted and creaky,
Lies a stanza that's cheeky and sneaky.
It sings in a tune,
Like a mischievous moon,
Sparking giggles from people all weeky.

With laughter it grows in the dark,
Each line is a spark of a lark.
A tickle on page,
Like mischief on stage,
It flies with a wink and a quark.

The rhymes are a goblin's delight,
They playfully chase off the night.
Each verse is a game,
With nonsense to claim,
That fills all the hearts with pure light.

So remember, it's all in the jest,
These verses are truly the best.
With laughter in mind,
You may just find,
The silliness locked in my chest.

Secrets Scribbled in Shadows

In the dim of a corner, quite sly,
Lies a secret that giggles can't die.
With a whisper of prose,
It merrily goes,
Each line with a wink to comply.

Beneath layers of dust and of cheer,
The scribbles invite all who can hear.
They dance with a twist,
In a whimsical mist,
Creating a world oh so dear.

Like echoes of laughter so light,
These verses take wing in the night.
With pranks and with fun,
They twist and they run,
Bringing joy in a delightful flight.

So peek into shadows with glee,
And let all your worries just be.
Those secrets concealed,
With laughter revealed,
Will bring all your giggles to spree.

The Vault of Rhyme

In a vault where the rhythms reside,
Lies a treasure of laughs, oh so wide.
With puns and with cheer,
And giggles so near,
It's a wild rollercoaster ride.

Each couplet a gem, shiny and bold,
Stories of antics quietly told.
They leap and they dance,
In a comical trance,
As delight in each stanza unfolds.

With giggles that echo like bells,
And riddles that tickle like elves,
The verses will burst,
With humor rehearsed,
Creating a laughter that swells.

So come take a peek, if you dare,
Unlocking the vault is a rare flair.
With rhymes on parade,
And gags on display,
A treasure of chuckles to share.

The Laughter in the Limelight

In a space where odd things collide,
A banana and briefcase reside.
They snicker and share,
In secret, they care,
For giggles and chuckles applied.

A frog in a hat, singing tunes,
While juggling three clumsy raccoons.
The crowd gasps in cheer,
As they gather so near,
To dance with the funny cartoons.

A sandwich that whispers a joke,
To a cat who can't help but invoke.
They cackle and roar,
Then tumble to floor,
While rolling around in their cloak.

As the laughter just fills up the air,
In this nook, it's a grand affair.
With a wink and a twist,
Nothing's amiss,
In this corner of joy, we all share.

Unseen Lines of Laughter

Behind doorways where shadows reside,
Lies a treasure, a giggling guide.
With silly old socks,
And chicken-shaped clocks,
All frolicking merrily inside.

A turtle with roller-skate wheels,
Whispers secrets of cakes and of meals.
With a flip and a spin,
The fun just begins,
Revealing the truth that it steals.

An octopus wears a bow tie,
Making everyone laugh till they cry.
With funny old puns,
And great prancing runs,
Joy floats like balloons to the sky.

Through the cracks where the sunlight beams,
Quirky wonders fulfill all our dreams.
With giggles galore,
And laughter's pure roar,
In this realm of delight, nothing seems.

Chronicles of the Concealed

Within crannies where secrets do fester,
Live a wizard who laughs like a jester.
With a flick of his wand,
He conjures a pond,
Full of fish jesting, playful, and luster.

A rubber duck dressed as a king,
Proclaims with a quack, it's a swing.
Upon throne made of dough,
He'll steal every show,
With the joy that his merry reign brings.

Suddenly, a puppet appears,
With jokes that bring forth laughter and cheers.
Her antics delight,
In the soft, golden light,
As she skips and she dances, no fears.

In this chamber of whimsy and play,
Hidden wonders abound day by day.
With folly in store,
And giggles galore,
Life's antics continue to sway.

Fantasies in Fragments

In a nook where oddities dwell,
A cactus who giggles, oh well!
He tells tales at night,
With underpants bright,
As whispers of laughter do swell.

A mouse with a cheery top hat,
Waltzes with a sleepy old cat.
Their steps are a dance,
In a comical trance,
As they twirl to the beat, imagine that!

With ice cream that sings silly tunes,
And a piano shaped like a moon.
They play jokes to the stars,
Making dreams feel like cars,
As they zoom through the whimsical dunes.

In this chamber of laughter and cheer,
Fragments of joy wander near.
With mirth all around,
New wonders are found,
As our worries just fade and disappear.

Limerick Lore from Within

There once was a sock full of cheese,
It danced with the wind and the breeze.
A mouse joined the fun,
But the cheese came undone,
Now it's stuck in a locker with peas.

A pencil that scribbles in rhyme,
Claims it knows secrets of time.
It whispers at night,
With dreams taking flight,
As erasers all gather to chime.

Tales Tangled in Tangles

A shoelace that ties up a tale,
Of when it tried sailing a whale.
But the knot was too tight,
And gave such a fright,
Now it's stuck with a frog in the gale.

An old rubber band made of fun,
Started bouncing and leaping to run.
It twisted and turned,
And the laughter it earned,
Is still echoing 'round in the sun.

Curiosities of the Steel Case

A sandwich once hid from the bread,
With pickles and mustard, it sped.
It peeked through the crack,
And with a loud whack,
Claimed it's better off eaten instead.

A compass that spun with a joke,
Said a map is just full of smoke.
It pointed to cheese,
With laughter and ease,
As the locker began to provoke.

The Poetry of Forgotten Spaces

In corners where dust bunnies lay,
A sock puppet dreams of the day.
It sings of a fight,
With a shoe far too bright,
And vows to never be led astray.

A crumpled old paper with notes,
Holds the musings of silly old goats.
They sing with delight,
In the blink of the night,
And the laughter just merrily floats.

www.ingramcontent.com/pod-product-compliance
Ingram Content Group UK Ltd.
Pitfield, Milton Keynes, MK11 3LW, UK
UKHW021136310125
454312UK00021B/50

9 783690 741729